D1557071

THE CROSS WAS THEIR BOOK

André Cirino, OFM

The Cross Was Their Book

Book design: Tau Publishing
Cover design: Jona and Josef Raischl, SFO
Cover image: Franciscan pilgrim Deborah Schumm
        Mt. LaVerna, Tuscany, Italy
Photography: from Franciscan pilgrims over many years

For information regarding permissions, write to:
Tau Publishing
Permissions Dept.
1422 East Edgemont Avenue
Phoenix, AZ 85006

ISBN-10:1-935257-19-6
ISBN-13: 978-1-935257-19-6

First Edition: January 2010
10 9 8 7 6 5 4 3 2 1

For re-orders and other inspirational books and materials visit our website at *Tau-Publishing.com*

Published and printed in the USA by:

Tau-Publishing.com
Words and Works of Inspiration

Acknowledgements

We are very grateful for permission to quote material printed by the following:

Reprinted by permission of Franciscan Institute Publications, The Franciscan Institute, St. Bonaventure University, St. Bonaventure, New York 14778, excerpts from "Divine Praise and Meditation according to the Teaching and Example of St. Francis of Assisi" in *Grayfriars Review,* Vol. 4, No. 1, 1990; *Clare of Assisi: Early Documents*, Regis Armstrong OFM Cap, 1993; *St. Francis and the Song of Brotherhood and Sisterhood*, Eric Doyle OFM, 1997; *The Geste of the Great King: Office of the Passion of Francis of Assisi*, Laurent Gallant OFM and André Cirino OFM, 2001; *Franciscan Solitude*, André Cirino OFM and Josef Raischl SFO, 1995.

Reprinted with permission of St. Anthony Messenger Press, 28 W. Liberty St., Cincinnati, OH 45202, www.sampbooks.org, excerpts from *Saint Francis of Assisi: Omnibus of Sources:* Volumes One and Two, copyright 2008, edited by Marion A. Habig; *The Journey into God: A Forty-Day Retreat with Bonaventure, Francis and Clare,* copyright 2002 by Josef Raischl, S.F.O. and André Cirino, O.F.M.

Reprinted with permission of Murray Bodo OFM, excerpts from *Clare, A Light in the Garden,*1992. Reprinted with permission of Damien Isabell OFM, excerpt from *Workbook for Franciscan Studies,* 1979.

Scripture citations are taken from *New Revised Standard Version: Study Bible,* Verlyn Verbrugge, ed., Grand Rapids, Michigan: Zondervan Publishing House, 1991 and *The New American Bible,* New York: Thomas Nelson Inc., 1971.

*This book is dedicated to
the third generation of our family:*

*River Lee Godbee
Knox Christian Theus
Cole Joseph Corraini
Jack Michael Corraini
Isabella Maria Theus
Greyson Eli Iorio
Emma Josephine Corraini
Sydney Theresa Iorio
Foster James Iorio*

*and their grandmother,
Angela Marie Cirino.*

CONTENTS

Introduction   5

Light   11

Faith   23

Hope   33

Love   45

The Will of God   59

Conclusion   73

Endnotes   74

.

Introduction

Anyone who tries to write about any aspect of the life of St. Francis faces the almost insurmountable obstacle of the eight centuries that have passed since he lived and died in Assisi. Nevertheless, there is a mountain of source material that we have inherited from Francis himself and his followers down through the ages. And within the collection of these sources, we find a pithy prayer composed and recited by St. Francis, simply known as his *Prayer Before a Crucifix*.

We read in St. Bonaventure's *Major Life of St. Francis*:

> There [at Rivotorto] they spent their time praying continuously. They prayed more from the heart than with the lips, since they did not yet possess any liturgical books from which to chant the Office. Rather, *the cross of Christ was their book*, and they studied it day and night at the exhortation and after the example of their father, who never ceased exhorting them about the cross.[1]

Whenever Francis went into solitude with the brothers, they would spend much time in prayer and meditation. However, not having any liturgical books in the early years, they would take two branches of a tree and mount them together in the form of a cross such as the cross from *sasso spicco* at LaVerna where Francis prayed in solitude. And it is on this symbol of Christ's suffering and death that Francis and his brothers as well as Clare and her sisters would focus their prayer — their meditation and contemplation.

More than likely Francis would have recited his brief prayer before the famous Crucifix of San Damiano, or perhaps used it whenever he found himself before any crucifix. The text that has come down to us in his language reads:

Most High, glorious God,	Altissimo glorioso dio,
enlighten	illumina
the darkness of my heart	le tenebre de lo core mio
and give me	et da me
right faith,	fede dricta,
certain hope,	sperança certa
and perfect charity,	et caritate perfecta,
sense and knowledge, Lord,	senno et cognoscemento, signore,
that I may do	che faça
Your holy and true	lo tuo santo e verace
command.	commandamento.[2]

The only type of crucifix that Francis and Clare would have known in the thirteenth century was a painted crucifix, of which there are a few extant in Assisi from that same era. According to Laurent Gallant, "Francis and Clare were only acquainted with the type of crucifix in the style of the Crucifix of San Damiano. The crucifixes they knew were in iconographic form. They never knew the crucifix with only a three-dimensional corpus on it which emerged in the 14th century."[3] Because of this, one can easily understand why so much has been studied, written and published in the form of books, videos, compact disks, etc., on the icon we call the Crucifix of San Damiano. If we want to appreciate the spirituality of Saints Francis and Clare, then it would be important to understand the art which influenced their spiritual lives. It was before these painted crucifixes that they prayed and meditated.

This book, however, focuses not on the art work itself, but on the prayer that St. Francis would have uttered when he sat before one of these masterpieces. This book has been prepared as a series of meditations on several themes drawn from his so-called *Prayer Before a Crucifix.*

Before I explain the contents of the book itself, it may be helpful first to share some thoughts about meditation in the life of St. Francis. In an article by a Capuchin friar, Octavian Schmucki treats of *Meditation in the Spirit of St. Francis of Assisi* from four considerations.

First, writing of the nature of Francis' meditation, Schmucki says that for Francis, "meditation means nothing else but the blissful savoring of the divine presence within."[4]

Second, in order to meditate on the divine presence within, Schmucki notes that the principal source for Francis was Holy Scripture, especially the Gospel of the day. Brother Leo penned this personal note in Francis' Breviary:

> [Francis] also had this book of the Gospels [with the readings for the liturgical seasons and the feasts of the saints] copied out, because whenever sickness or other obstacles prevented him from hearing Mass, he had the Gospel of the day read to him. He continued this practice to the day of his death.[5]

Third, Schmucki suggests a method for St. Francis' meditation which could be summarized as follows:

> 1. For Francis the first stage of prayer meant a determined effort to break loose from the multiple so as to be united with the One . . . The Poverello had recourse to a variety of means to promote and safeguard recollection—isolated places . . . silence . . . avoid useless and especially uncharitable talk. . . . striving toward inner peace.
> 2. A second step he took to achieve complete detachment was to repent of past sins and failings.
> 3. Francis then adds some reflection on a text from the Bible, on some divine mystery, on some encounter of the day.[6]

And fourth, Schmucki treats of the *fruits* of Francis' meditation, the results this type of prayer had in his life and preaching.

This book centers on five themes found in this *Prayer Before a Crucifix*, namely, the themes of Light, Faith, Hope, Love and the Will of God. These themes animated Francis' prayer whenever he sat before a crucifix and they would have been for him a deep well from which to draw living water that nourished his meditation. So I have expanded each theme with one or more stories from the Franciscan sources which help illustrate the topic under consideration accompanied by my own reflection or meditation on each one.

At the end of each section there are suggestions to assist you in your own meditation guided by Schmucki's thoughts above. Since Holy Scripture was the main source of Francis' meditation, biblical passages are given for each of the five themes. Schmucki also noted that Francis meditated on the divine mysteries, so I have recommended some divine mysteries which seem to connect with each theme. And finally, Francis reflected on encountering God in his daily experience. This becomes the challenge for each of us as we try to discover how we personally incarnate in ourselves each of the themes of Francis' *Prayer Before a Crucifix.*

Deep below the dwelling of St. Francis on Mount LaVerna
is a projecting rock, *sasso spicco*,
where tradition says that Francis would have meandered down
to spend solitude time in prayer.
This cross is an example of the type of cross
that became their book, their light in the early years.

Light

Saint Francis prayed:

Enlighten   *illumina*
the darkness of my heart   *le tenebre de lo core mio*

****

A reading from *The Little Flowers of St. Francis:*

When St. Francis was staying in Assisi, he often visited St Clare and consoled her with holy advice. And as she had a very great desire to eat a meal with him once, she asked him several times to give her that consolation. But St. Francis always refused to grant her that favor. So it happened that his companions, perceiving St. Clare's desire, said to St. Francis: "Father, it seems to us that this strictness is not according to divine charity—that you do not grant the request of Sister Clare, a virgin so holy and dear to God, in such a little thing as eating with you, especially considering that she gave up the riches and pomp of the world as a result of your preaching. So you should not only let her eat a meal with you once, but if she were to ask an even greater favor of you, you should grant it to your little spiritual plant."

St. Francis answered: "So you think I should grant this wish of hers?" And the companions said: "Yes, Father, for she deserves this favor and consolation." Then St. Francis replied: "Since it seems so to you, I agree. But in order to give her greater pleasure, I want this meal to be at St. Mary of the Angels, for she has been cloistered at San Damiano for a long time and she will enjoy seeing once more for a while the Place of St. Mary where she was shorn and made a spouse of the Lord Jesus Christ. So we will eat there together, in the name of the Lord." He therefore set a day when St. Clare would go out of the monastery with one sister companion, escorted also by his companions.

And she came to St. Mary of the Angels. And first she reverently and humbly greeted the Blessed Virgin Mary before her altar, where she had been shorn and received the veil. And then they devoutly showed her around the Place until it was mealtime. Meanwhile St. Francis had the table prepared on the bare ground, as was his custom. And when it was time to eat, St. Francis and St. Clare sat down together, and one of his companions with St. Clare's companion, and all his other companions were grouped around that humble table. But at the first course St. Francis began to speak about God in such a sweet and holy and profound and divine and marvelous way that he himself and St. Clare and her companion and all the others who were at that poor little table were rapt in God by the overabundance of divine grace that descended upon them.

And while they were sitting there, in a rapture, with their eyes and hands raised to Heaven, it seemed to the men of Assisi and Bettona and the entire district that the Church of St. Mary of the Angels and the whole Place and the forest which was at that time around the Place were all *aflame and that an immense fire was burning* over all of them. Consequently the men of Assisi ran down there in great haste to save the Place and put out the fire, as they firmly believed that everything was burning up. But when they reached the Place, they saw that nothing was on fire. Entering the Place, they found St. Francis with St. Clare and all the companions sitting around that very humble table, rapt in God by contemplation and invested with power from on high. Then *they knew for sure that it had been a heavenly and not a material fire that God had miraculously shown them to symbolize the fire of divine love which was burning in the souls of those holy friars and nuns.* So they withdrew, with great consolation in their hearts and with holy edification.

Later, after a long while, when St. Francis and St. Clare and the others came back to themselves, they felt so refreshed by spiritual food that they paid little or no attention to the material food. And when that blessed meal was over, St. Clare, well accompanied, returned to San Damiano. The sisters were very glad to see her.[1]

****

When my niece was pregnant with the beginning of a new generation in our family, I was visiting with her one day and asked her by what name she intended to call her child. She already knew that she would birth a baby boy and she was thinking of naming the child either Zachary or Jake. When her son was born on 11 April, I telephoned my niece and asked what name she had chosen. She responded that they decided to name him River.

When I share this with people, there's usually a muffled reaction in the audience. Then I read them the following from an early biography of St. Clare:

> While the pregnant woman [St. Clare's mother], already near delivery, was attentively praying to the Crucified before the cross in a church to bring her safely through the danger of childbirth, she heard a voice saying to her:
> *"Do not be afraid, woman, for you will give birth in safety to a light which will give light more clearly than light itself."*
> Taught by this oracle, when the child was born and then reborn in sacred Baptism, *she ordered that she be called Chiara, hoping that the brightness of the promised light would in some way be fulfilled according to the divine pleasure. Hardly had she been brought into the light, than the little Chiara began to shine sufficiently in the darkness of the world and to be resplendent.*[2]

After hearing this birth/naming story, there's no muffled reaction, usually just a devout silence in the audience. And yet, in reality, Ortolana named her firstborn child "Light." Perhaps we've become so accustomed to this name—Chiara/Clare—that the true meaning is lost to us. But the meaning was not lost to the person who composed the official document the Vatican issues for a person's canonization. Take a look at the lines excerpted from St. Clare's papal canonization document of 1255 which play on her name meaning "Light":

> Clare
> shines brilliantly,
> brilliant by her bright merits,
> By the brightness of her great glory in heaven,
> and by the brilliance of her sublime miracles on earth.
> Clare . . . radiates . . . glows. . . .
> The fullness of the divine light shines on her . . .
> bright . . . brighter . . . even brighter . . .
> brilliant in splendor. . . .
> O the ineffable brilliance of the blessed Clare . . .
> resplendent . . . enlightened as a radiant beam in her home,
> dazzled as lightning in the enclosure.
> She shone forth in life,
> she is radiant after death.
> Enlightening on earth,
> she dazzles in heaven.
> O how great is the power of this light
> and how intense is the brilliance of its illumination . . .
> emitted sparkling rays outside. . . .
> It should not be surprising that a light so enkindled,
> so illuminating could not be kept from shining brilliantly
> and giving clear light in the house of the Lord.[3]

In his *Prayer Before a Crucifix,* St. Francis prays God to "Enlighten the darkness of my heart." Chiara—St. Clare—personifies this light in her heart. And St. Francis does as well.

It is worth noting that the Prologue to the *Legend of the Three Companions* compares Francis himself to the sun which he loved and revered so much: *'Resplendent as the dawn and as the morning star, or even as the rising sun, setting the world alight, cleansing it, giving it fertility, Francis was seen to rise as a new kind of light."* St. Bonaventure in the Prologue to his *Major Life of St. Francis* is a little more circumspect:

> He was to be a *light* for those who believe that, *by bearing witness of the light,* he might prepare a way for the Lord to the hearts of his faithful, a way of light and peace. By the *glorious splendor of his life and teaching, Francis shone like the daystar amid the clouds, and by the brilliance which radiated from him, he guided those who live in darkness, in the shadow of death, to the light.*[4]

Francis and Clare are the seraphic ones—which means the burning ones. They both were on fire with love—a love of God, of neighbor, of self and of creation. That's what the opening story from the *Little Flowers of St. Francis* is all about. The people from Assisi and the surrounding area came to what they thought was an "immense fire" ready to put out the flames. But they quickly realized that it was "the fire of divine love which was burning in the souls of those holy friars and nuns." And it is precisely this fire that burned in them that has drawn and still attracts millions of pilgrims to their tombs in Assisi.

Murray Bodo wrote of Clare: "And then she heard Francis preach. The words were simple and unadorned, but they touched her like a deep and purifying shaft of light. *Her whole being seemed bathed in a light that came from somewhere inside her own heart.*"[5]

There is a little book published in Assisi called *The Little Flowers of Saint Clare.* A few excerpts from some of the stories illustrate how the sisters saw this same fire burning in their Mother Clare. One story begins: "Back at San Damiano Clare continued to *shed light* around her."[6] The sisters saw this light simply from living with this woman. In her *Third Letter to St. Agnes of Prague,* St. Clare wrote: "Do not let bitterness wrap itself around you like a cloud."[7] Clouds block the light. Clare knew that bitterness would extinguish the flame of love that burned in her heart. So she warned Agnes to beware of such bitterness in her life struggles. Moreover, when one meets persons who shed light around themselves, our own spark of light within is ignited into flame that others can easily see.

Regarding her prayer life, the sisters saw that "when she returned after praying, her face seemed *clearer* and *more resplendent than the sun.*"[8] This has overtones to Exodus 34:29 when "Moses came down from Mount Sinai. . . . Moses did not know that the skin of his face shone because he had been talking with God." This was a similar experience for the sisters in Clare's monastery at San Damiano.

Francis knew this as well about Clare. "Far from her Francis prayed that *her light might shine ever clearer* before all. Standing in prayer during the night, he raised his eyes to the stars and asked the Lord to let the Poor Ladies *shine with splendor even as those heavenly bodies.*"[9] Another time when Francis was conversing with Brother Leo who wondered what Francis saw as he gazed for a long time into the shaft of a well, Francis responded: "Brother Leo, I saw the face of our Sister Clare who I thought was suffering and under temptation. Instead she was all peace and *brightness.*"[10]

In the *Canticle of the Creatures* Francis uses the word *clarite* for describing the moon and the stars. The obvious translation of the word is "clear" with overtones for the name Clare. One of my professors in Rome said he checked all available lexicons in that city, and this particular meaning for *clarite* was not found. Did Francis use it originally, purposely with Clare in mind? Moreover, Francis wrote the *Canticle of the Creatures* towards the end of his life when he was blind, almost, one can say, composing from "insight." Occasionally I had the privilege of celebrating Eucharist in the home of Elise, a blind woman in her 90s. Physically she sat in darkness, yet when one listened to her, it was so easy to tell that her life was full of light!

From the writings of Clare it may be conjectured that she may have been familiar with this prayer of Francis. In her *Testament* she wrote: "After the most high heavenly Father saw fit in His mercy and grace to *enlighten my heart,* that I should do penance according to the example and teaching of our most blessed father Francis . . . "[11] And in her Rule Clare wrote: "As long as she [the sister in question] remains obstinate, let them pray that the Lord will *enlighten her heart* to do penance."[12]

So now, what meaning could this word *light* carry for us? Jesus said: "I am the light of the world" [John 8:12]. Since Jesus is this light of the world, then this light, this burning fire is divine. In Matthew's Gospel, Jesus says: "You are the light of the world" [Matthew 5:14]. This divine light, which Jesus says we are, is in us!

But how does one know that one walks in the light? Ephesians 5:8-14 endeavors to respond to this question:

> For you were once darkness,
> but now in the Lord you are light.
> Live as children of light
> for the fruit of the light is found
> in all that is good and right and true.
> Try to find out what is pleasing to the Lord.
> Take no part in the unfruitful works of darkness,
> but instead expose them.
> For it is shameful even to mention what such people do secretly;
> but everything exposed by the light becomes visible,
> for everything that becomes visible is light.
> Therefore it says:
> "Sleeper, awake!
> Rise from the dead, and Christ will shine on you."

So when our lives reflect all that is "good and right and true," we are walking as people of the light, God as it were, shining through us because God is "all that is good and right and true." We are filled with the seraphic fire that burned in Francis and Clare. We have the divine energy, power, flame that must be put "on the lampstand" that "your light shine before others, so that they may see your good works and give glory to your Father in heaven" [*Matthew* 5:15-16].

The mystics' doctrine of *synteresis* is the idea that divine sparks exist in every human being waiting to be ignited into flame. Murray Bodo wrote of Clare:

> Jesus, always Jesus, *smoldering in her heart, then flaming up suddenly,* surprising her with the ardor of his love. No matter how intensely she looked to Francis for teaching and guidance, for friendship and fraternity, he never replaced Jesus as Lord and master of her heart and soul. And Jesus proved over and over again his love for her. Always, even when she was beginning to despair of his love, he would return suddenly, unexpectedly, *the warmth of his entry as soft as the morning sun upon the white roses of her little garden.* Her Lord always seemed to know when his seeming distance was causing havoc in her heart. She would turn inward and pray aloud in her anguish, begging Jesus to come to her and fill the void. And the Lord would remain silent and away.
>
> Then, when she was not praying but working in her garden, or nursing her sick sisters, or working at her sewing, it would happen—*with a sudden rush of warmth* he would be there, saving her again, rewarding her patience with his presence and the power of his healing. And he would seem to *come from within as if he had in fact been smoldering in*

her heart with just enough spark to be re-enkindled by the Spirit—that Spirit like the wind, blowing where it would and refusing to be harnessed by any magic formula of prayer.

Slowly she learned to wait upon the Lord and his Spirit, to open her mind and heart like thirsty ground waiting for rain, like rose petals *waiting for the sun.* And if she waited in patience and continued to work faithfully at whatever was at hand, the Lord would always surprise her, sometimes meeting her in the kitchen, sometimes in the laundry, sometimes in the refectory, sometimes even when she was sweeping the earthen floor with nothing particular on her mind.[13]

To conclude these reflections, in his masterpiece *The Journey of the Human Person into God,* St. Bonaventure climbed Mount LaVerna for forty days to reconnect with God's presence in his life. And one of the symbols he uses for himself in this manuscript is the light that we experience in the course of a day.[14]

When Bonaventure looks for God outside himself in creation, he picks up vestiges of God and compares this experience of the vestiges of God's presence to the light of dusk. The light is there at dusk—it is fading—but it is, nevertheless, perceptible. When Bonaventure looks for God inside himself, he experiences God's presence through his inner faculties and in grace, calls these images of God, stronger than the vestiges, and compares them to the light of dawn, a light that constantly grows stronger and stronger.

And finally, when Bonaventure looks for God's presence beyond himself in two names used for God—in Being itself and in the Good—he claims these are the strongest experiences, calls them similitudes or likenesses of God, and compares them to the blinding light of noon. These are illuminations that St. Bonaventure experienced, urging and exhorting us to pay attention to the same.

To assist you in your meditation:

1. Like St. Francis, meditate on the Scripture readings or just the Gospel of the day, or on a text from the Bible. Some suggestions on this theme of Light are:

> Matthew 5:14
>
> John 1:5; 8:12; 9:5; 12:46.
>
> 1 John 1:5, 7; 2:7-10; 3:2.

2. Again, like St. Francis, meditate on some divine mystery. Using the Crucifix of San Damiano, focus yourself on the luminous body of Jesus on the cross who proclaimed: "I am the light of the world" [John 8:12], and consider the Incarnation, the birth of this Light, or his Transfiguration, or his Resurrection from the dead.

3. St. Francis also meditated on meeting God/Jesus in some encounter of the day. What is your experience or encounter today with the Light of the world?

Both saints, Francis and Clare, prayed
before this Crucifix of San Damiano.
In prayer, Francis heard the decisive challenge
to rebuild the Church;
in contemplation, Clare gazed into this mirror daily
as a spouse of Jesus Christ.
Their faith was riveted on this icon.

Faith

Saint Francis prayed:

and give me	*et da me*
right faith	*fede dricta*

****

A reading from the *Mirror of Perfection:*

The most blessed Father, having in some degree transformed the friars into saints by his burning love and by the fervent zeal for their perfection which fired him, often pondered on the virtues that ought to adorn a *good friar minor.* He used to say that a good friar minor should imitate the lives and possess the merits of these holy friars: the *perfect faith* and love of poverty of Brother Bernard.[1]

A reading from *The Little Flowers of St. Francis:*

Among them the first-born, both by priority of time and privilege of sanctity, was Brother Bernard of Quintavalle, whose conversion took place in the following way.

St. Francis was still dressed as a layman, although he had already renounced the world, and for a long time he had been going around Assisi looking contemptible and so mortified by penance that many people thought he was simple-minded, and he was laughed at as a lunatic and driven away with many insults and stones and mud by his relatives and by strangers. Yet being nourished by the divine salt and firmly established in peace of soul by the Holy Spirit, he bore all the insults and scorn with great patience and with a joyful expression on his face.

Now Bernard, who was one of the richest and wisest nobles in the whole city, whose judgment everyone respected, began to think over St. Francis' utter contempt for the world and his great patience when he was insulted and the fact that, although he had been scorned and despised by everybody for two years, he always appeared more serene and patient. Bernard began to think and say to himself: "This Francis certainly must have great graces from God."

So inspired by God, he invited St. Francis to have supper with him that evening. Francis accepted. Bernard secretly wished and planned to put St. Francis' holiness to a test, so he invited him to sleep in his house that night. And when St. Francis agreed, Bernard had a bed prepared in his own room, in which a lamp was always kept burning at night.

Now St. Francis, as soon as he entered the room, in order to conceal the divine graces which he had, immediately threw himself down on the bed, showing that he wished to sleep. But Bernard planned to watch him secretly during the night. And he too soon lay down, and he used such cunning that after he had rested in bed a while, he pretended to be sleeping soundly, and he began to snore loudly.

When St. Francis thought that Bernard was fast asleep, he got out of bed and began to pray. Looking up to heaven and raising his hands, he prayed with intense fervor and devotion saying: "My God and my all!" And he sobbed out those words with so many tears and kept repeating them with such devout persistence that until matins he said nothing but "My God and my all!"

Now Bernard saw the very inspiring actions of St. Francis by the light of the lamp burning there. And while he was meditating on the words which Francis was saying and noting his devotion, he was touched by the Holy Spirit in the depths of his heart and felt inspired to change his life. Therefore, when morning came, he called St. Francis and said to him: "Brother Francis, I have resolved in my heart to leave the world and follow you in whatever you order me to do."

When St. Francis heard this, he rejoiced in spirit and said: "Lord Bernard, what you say is so great and difficult an undertaking that we must seek the advice of Our Lord Jesus Christ concerning it, so that He Himself may deign to show us His will regarding it and teach us how we should carry it out. So let us go together to church; and as the Lord taught his disciples, we will learn from the book of the Gospel what to do."

They rose early; and with another man named Peter Catanii, who also wished to join them, they went to the church of St. Nicholas near the chief square of the city. They went in to pray, but being simple men, they did not know how to find the passage in the Gospel telling of the renunciation of the world. Therefore, they asked God to show them God's will the first time they opened the book. When their prayer was ended, Francis, kneeling before the altar, took the closed book, opened it and saw written: "If you wish to be perfect, go, sell what you have, and give to the poor, and you shall have treasure in heaven" [Matthew 19:21]. At this Blessed Francis gave thanks to God with great joy; but because of his devotion to the Blessed Trinity, he desired a threefold confirmation of the words and opened the book of the Gospel a second and a third time. At the second opening he read: "Take nothing for your journey, no walking staff, no traveling bag, no bread, no money" [Luke 9:3]; and at the third: "If any will come after me, let them deny themselves, take up their cross, and follow Me" [Matthew 16:24]. Each time he opened the book blessed Francis gave thanks to God for this threefold confirmation of the resolution and desire which he had long held in his heart; and he said to Bernard and Peter: "O Brothers, this is our life and rule and the life and rule of all those who may wish to join us. Go and act on what you have heard."

So Master Bernard, who was very rich, sold all his possessions, and distributed a great deal of money to the poor of the city. Peter too, according to his means, followed our Lord's counsel.[2]

****

In his *Prayer Before a Crucifix* St. Francis asks his "Most High, Glorious God" for the gift of a "right" or a "correct faith." We shall speak of his chosen adjective shortly, but first let us look at the notion of faith itself.

As an experience in our lives, faith is like a process whereby one *accepts* something which is *partly seen* and *partly unseen,* and *risks* accepting the reality as *true.* Sitting in your home looking out the windows on a beautiful day filled with brilliant sunshine, you can tell yourself, "I *know* the sun is shining." You wouldn't say, "I believe the sun is shining," because the data is right before you streaming in through your windows. However, if you were for several hours in a part of your home that was windowless, you would not be able to say, "I *know* the sun is shining," because of a lack of data. You could risk saying, "I *believe* the sun is shining." Data in the form of that which is seen is part of the process of faith. But there is more.

You can be traveling on a city train sitting next to a stranger. This is the data that is seen. What is *unseen* is wide open: will the stranger remain calm throughout the trip or possibly become verbally or physically abusive? You don't know this as you sit next to someone in a public place. In fact, using the same example, will you get off the train with your wallet or purse? While it's an *accepted truth* that you may need public transportation—that which is seen, what is *unseen* is: will the train ride be made safely, without incident or not? But since you need transportation, you take a *risk* and use the train.

In light of our discussion thus far, we can now take a look at the faith of Brother Bernard. First, what was the data that Bernard was considering? He saw Francis in Assisi being insulted by mud and stones thrown at him, mocked and ridiculed verbally by his family as well as by strangers, all the while maintaining a joyful patience. Bernard personally tested the truth of Francis' new way of life by observing him as he prayed throughout the night. And this data touched Bernard in the core of his being. That's the *accepted reality* or *truth* that was *seen* by Bernard. What was *unseen* by Bernard was whether he himself could live the same way. And when he decided to *risk* all after hearing the Scriptures at the church of St. Nicholas, his faith sustaind him, giving him the strength to act on what he heard and believed.

To deepen our notion of faith, let us look at the familiar passage in Matthew 14:22-31:

> Immediately he made the disciples get into the boat and go on ahead to the other side, while he dismissed the crowds. And after he had dismissed them, he went up the mountain by himself to pray. When evening came, he was there alone, but by this time the boat, battered by the waves, was far from the land for the wind was against them.
> And early in the morning he came walking toward them on the sea. But when the disciples saw him walking on the sea, they were terrified saying, "It is a ghost!" And they cried out in fear.
> But immediately Jesus spoke to them and said, "Take heart, it is I; do not be afraid."
> Peter answered him, "Lord, if it is you, command me to come out to you on the water."
> He said, "Come."
> *So Peter got out of the boat, started walking on the water, and came toward Jesus.* But when he noticed the strong wind, he became frightened, and beginning to sink, he cried out, "Lord, save me!" Jesus immediately reached out his hand and caught him, saying to him "You of little faith, why did you doubt?"

In light of the above passage, let us look at Peter's faith. What is seen by Peter is Jesus walking on the water towards him. That was the *accepted reality* before him. What is *unseen* by Peter is whether he could do the same. Jesus invites Peter to come to him on the water.

Now Peter's home was Capernaum, on the northern shore of the Sea of Galilee. As a child, his mother would have brought him to the edge of the lake warning him that should he go into it, he would sink! Now with Jesus' invitation and his mother's advice ringing in his ears, Peter *risked* putting his foot over the side of the boat and started to walk on the water towards Jesus. This certainly must have amazed this fisherman. But when Peter noticed the wind and waves of the storm, he began to sink. His faith sustained him as long as he kept his eyes fixed on Jesus. As soon as he looked at the data of the storm, he switched from the process of believing to a new process of doubting, dealing with the data before him. Moving to a new process of doubting had the effect of Peter beginning to sink. Nevertheless, he did walk on the water a bit!

This movement from believing to doubting in Peter raises the question of choice. In every experience of life, be it discernment of one's future or a present crisis, we always have the choice as to where we place our energy—do we place it in a process of faith with the risk that entails, or do we place it in a process of doubting which leaves us in abeyance with the data at hand? Deuteronomy 30:19 challenges us to "choose life."

When I have presented this example to an audience, I usually ask them at this point: from 0-100 pounds, how much faith did Peter need to walk on the water? Someone invariably responds—100 pounds! For it seems so miraculous, certainly beyond human potential. But actually, how much faith was necessary? We read in Matthew 17:20 Jesus saying, "For truly I tell you, if you have faith the size of a mustard seed, you will say to this mountain, 'Move from here to there' and it will move; and nothing will be impossible for you." Mountains could symbolize the obstacles in our lives, and by faith of a miniscule amount, Jesus is telling us we can deal with these problems. He goes even further with a statement that bolsters dreams, "Nothing will be impossible for you."

Where does faith come from? The teaching of the Church is that we are gifted with faith by God at our baptism. So faith is a gift! We are accustomed with the ritual of giving and receiving gifts in our lives. When we get a gift that we don't like, what happens to it? Usually, we leave it somewhere in our home, unused and unwanted. Or we may recycle it to someone else. But when we receive a gift that we like, we certainly use it and enjoy it as long as possible. This simple gift-ritual says much to us about the gift of faith. God gives it to us at baptism. If we were baptized as an infant, then we received the gift and had to be taught, hopefully by our parents or godparents, how to use the gift. But again, the choice to use it or not is certainly ours.

Moreover, I have frequently heard the statement made that someone has "lost his/her faith." If faith is a gift, I don't think it's possible to lose it. We can refuse to use it. That is certainly our choice. But it never disappears. It remains somewhere in the recesses of our spiritual being. And it remains there like a pilot light in a stove. We cannot cook a meal over a pilot light; it must be ignited into flame. So faith, like a spark within us, is always there, waiting for us to ignite it in order to face the struggles, crises and crosses of daily life.

Furthermore, faith is contagious. When we live with a person of demonstrable faith, somehow the fire that burns in the believer is transmitted to others in the same house or community. And such a fire of faith burns brighter and stronger with a light that cannot be hidden! And such a faith makes dreams a reality or bolsters our struggles and crises with a peace that passes understanding. In his *Prayer Before a Crucifix*, St. Francis prays for "right" or "correct faith." The Church of the early 13th century saw the emergence of poverty movements like the Waldensians or the Humiliati, as well as the followers of St. Francis and St. Dominic. Aside from the latter two, the other groups separated themselves from the Church. And perhaps in contrast with the poverty movements of his day which had a wrong/incorrect/heretical faith, Francis, by his obedience to the Church of Rome, not only maintained a "correct faith," but laid the foundation for situating his entire Order in the heart of the Church.

Finally, the symbol for faith is the cross. It seems that every time we are faced with significant decisions or problems and crises in our lives, we come face to face with the cross. And the risk each time for us is to pick up this cross with faith and then watch God do some marvelous deeds in our lives!

To assist you in your meditation:

1. Like St. Francis, meditate on the Scripture readings or just the Gospel of the day, or on a text from the Bible. Some suggestions are on this theme of faith are:

> Matthew 14:22-32; 15:21-28; 17:19-21
>
> Mark 15:39
>
> Hebrews 11

2. Again, like St. Francis, meditate on some divine mystery. Meditate with John the Beloved Disciple who rested on Jesus at the last supper. Meditate on the Eucharist instituted at this Passover meal and the risk that challenged the Apostles to believe this was now the body and blood of Jesus. Moreover, meditate on the risk of intimacy that John shared with Jesus that prefigures our intimate Eucharistic life.

3. St. Francis also meditated on meeting God/Jesus in some

encounter of the day. What is your experience or encounter today with the gift of faith? What was the unseen for you today that challenged you to risk by believing?

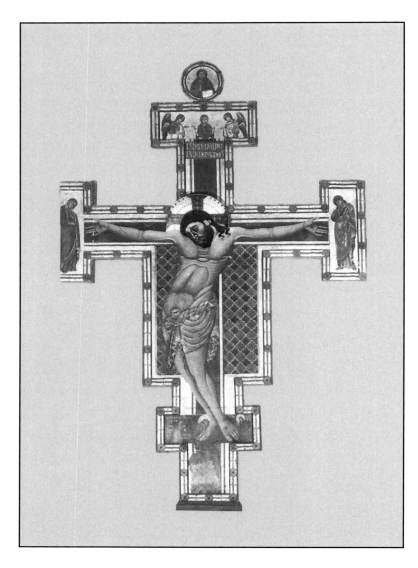

Hanging above the main altar in the Basilica of St. Clare
is this large crucifix depicting the *Christus Patiens*,
the suffering Christ,
who is our hope in trial, difficulty, sickness
or struggle of any kind.

Hope

and give me   *et da me*
firm hope   *sperança certa*

****

A reading from *The Little Flowers of St. Francis:*

A very delicate young man of noble birth entered the Order of St. Francis. A few days after he took the habit, through the instigation of the devil, he began to hate the habit he was wearing so much that he felt as though he was wearing a very course sack. The sleeves got on his nerves, he disliked the cowl, and the length and roughness of the habit seemed an unbearable burden to him. And so it happened that as his distaste for the Order increased, he finally resolved to throw the habit away and return to the world.

Now the novice director of this young man had taught him that when he passed in front of the altar of the friary in which the Blessed Sacrament was kept, he should kneel down, bow with hands crossed on his chest. And this the novice always carefully did.

And it happened on the night when he had decided to put aside the habit and leave the Order that he had to pass before the altar of the friary, and there he knelt and bowed. All of a sudden he was shown a marvelous vision by God.

He saw passing before him an almost countless throng of saints, two by two in procession, and they were dressed in precious vestments, their faces and hands and visible parts of their bodies were shining more radiantly than the sun. And they marched by, singing hymns, while angels were chanting their joy.

Among the saints there were two who were more splendidly dressed and surrounded by such brilliance that they dazzled anyone who looked at them. And almost at the end of the procession he saw one who was adorned with such glory that he seemed like a new knight being especially honored by the others.

When the young man saw this vision, he was amazed, but did not know what the procession meant. Yet he did not question those who were passing by, being overwhelmed with bliss. But when the whole procession had passed and he saw the last ones, he ran to them asking: "Who are those persons in this beautiful procession?"

They turned their radiant faces toward him and answered: "Son, all of us are Friars Minor who have just come from the glory of paradise." And he asked: "Who are those two who shine more brightly than the others?" "Those two are Sts. Francis and Anthony. And the last one whom you saw being so honored is a holy friar who recently died. Because he fought valiantly against temptations and persevered until the end, we are now conducting him in triumph and glory to the joy of paradise with the Saints as companions and the angels rejoicing. And these beautiful garments which we are wearing were given to us by God in exchange for the rough habits which we wore with *patience*. And the glorious radiance which you see in us was given to us by God for the humble penance, poverty, obedience and chastity which we observed to the end with *joyful* minds and faces. Therefore, son, it should not be hard for you to wear the 'sack' of such a fruitful Order because if, with the 'sack' of St. Francis and for the love of Jesus you despise the world and fight valiantly against the devil, you will likewise have a similar garment and will shine with us in glory."

And when they had said those words, the young man came back to himself. And encouraged by that vision, he rejected all temptation and acknowledged his fault before the guardian and the other friars. Henceforth, he longed for the roughness of penance and of the habit as if longing for wealth. And thus converted into a better man, he lived a very holy life and died in the Order, to the glory of Jesus Christ. Amen.[1]

****

In his *Prayer Before a Crucifix* St. Francis asks his "Most High, Glorious God" for the gift of "firm hope." Again, I shall speak of his chosen adjective later, but first let us look at the notion of hope itself.

When I reflect on the virtue of hope, the first Scripture that comes to mind is from the book of Romans 8, verses 24 and 25.

> In hope we were saved. But hope is not hope if its object is seen; how is it possible to hope for what one sees? And hoping for what we cannot see means *awaiting it with patient endurance.*

From the above quotation, it's clear that there are at least two important aspects of this virtue of hope: waiting and patience.

First, let's talk about waiting. We Americans love to wait! I say that with tongue-in-cheek because waiting is not easy for many people. Living in the New York City area for most of my adult life, I know that when I travel from one borough to another, I will have to cross one or more bridges, many of them with tolls to pay. I always aim my car for the shortest toll line, and am content when I succeed, except for the time when the driver in the car in front of me asks directions of the toll collector who has not spoken to anyone most of the day. Their conversation, though brief, seems endless and I'm fighting hard not to press my horn to keep them moving.

Waiting is an invitation for us to hold on, to hang in there for a while until things or situations resolve themselves. But there is so much in the American culture that militates against waiting—fast food places, instant coffees and teas, drive-by bank windows, etc. Moreover, it's interesting to note that the words for "hope" and "wait" in the languages below share the same root or stem—even the English word sometimes used for a woman who is pregnant/expecting, comes close!

sperare	to hope	Italian
esperar	to hope or to wait	Spanish
aspettare	to wait	Italian
expecting		English
sperança	hope	Francis' medieval language

Carroll Stuhlmueller writes: "Hope is identical with the virtue of waiting except that it adds a quality of optimism."[2] "[H]ave your lamps lit . . . waiting for [the] master to return," says Jesus [Luke 12:35-36]. It is our ability to wait that facilitates the second aspect of hope—patience.

The meaning of the word "patience" stems from the Latin patior, meaning I *suffer*. A person who enters a hospital with an ailment is usually referred to as a *patient*, one who is suffering. And suffering is an experience that exempts no one—suffering in small ways like the discomfort of hot, humid weather, or in more important ways such as the illness or death of a loved one. We have no choice but to suffer. However, we do have a choice as to *how* we suffer. I would like to suggest that our suffering can be experienced in a manner which is meaningful or meaningless. I can best explain these by example.

First, some thoughts about meaningful suffering. In one assignment as a parish associate, I had the responsibility to take the Eucharist to some of our people who were homebound. The first time I did this, I was given a list of names and addresses of about five people. I proceeded to my first call, a large tenement building. Looking at the list of names by the door, I pressed the bell and waited about two minutes before I was let in. I walked up to the second floor and knocked on the door. When the door opened, Eddie was lying on the floor, looking up at me, smiling with the greeting, "How are you Father?" Well, I was in shock! Usually when a door opens to let you in, you meet a person face-to-face. Eddie was lying on the floor because he was paralyzed from the waist down and the apartment was too small to allow wheelchair usage.

I watched Eddie slowly drag himself along the floor of the flat as he made his way to the kitchen and painfully hoist himself up on to a chair. Then he smiled again with a cascade of questions. "How's everyone at St. Mary's? How was the eleven o'clock mass last Sunday? How is the prayer meeting coming along?" I responded to each of his queries, watching the joy in the smiles on his face. Not once did Eddie complain to me. We were the same age. At that time I had already been using my legs for 41 years. Eddie had never used his legs because he was paralyzed from birth. In spite of this daily, constant suffering, there was joy in this man. Somehow, Eddie knew meaning in suffering.[3]

Although all of us suffer, for some, their suffering is devoid of meaning. When I was stationed at an inner city parish, a young man came running into the friary one evening to tell me that a teenager was unconscious in a vacant lot behind the church. After some quick questioning, I ran to the lot and discovered that the teenager had mixed alcohol with some drugs. I picked him up and got him to the local emergency room where he recovered after they pumped out the contents of his stomach. This teenager came from a large, dysfunctional family in the city projects—housing for the poor. In his own and somewhat life-threatening way he was trying to cope with the suffering that afflicts the poor. But he chose a way that led him to the suffering that endangered his health and existence—meaningless suffering.

Going back to the novice in the opening story, he was a "very delicate young man of noble birth," accustomed to fine clothing. The habit—"the 'sack' of St. Francis"—that he was given as a novice brought on a suffering he was not willing to endure. Instead of waiting, "hanging in there" in his initial training, he was preparing to leave the Order. But in the vision, the friar addressing him noted "the *joyful* minds and faces" of the friars and the one being honored in the heavenly procession—all of them dressed in beautiful garments as reward for wearing their "sack" of St. Francis with patience.

This little story brings up the element of joy in suffering. In his early years, St. Francis loathed lepers, claiming that the sight of them nauseated him, leaving him feeling bitter. But once he encountered a leper on the road and embraced him, then that which was bitter for him changed into a sweetness that permeated his entire being. In suffering, there was sweetness.

Whenever I'm with Franciscans and something goes wrong, someone always derisively remarks "perfect joy," alluding to the following story:

> One day at St. Mary of the Angels, St. Francis called Brother Leo and said: "Brother Leo, write this down." He answered: "I'm ready."
> "Write what true joy is. A messenger comes and says that all the masters of theology at the University of Paris have joined the Order—write: that is not true joy!
> "Or all the prelates beyond the Alps—archbishops and bishops, or the kings of France and England joined the Order—write: that is not true joy!
> "Or that my friars have gone to unbelievers and converted all of them to the faith; or that I have so much grace from God that I heal the sick and I perform many miracles. I tell you that true joy is not in all those things."

Brother Leo asked: "But what is true joy?"

"I am returning from Perugia and I am coming here at night in the dark. It is wintertime, wet and muddy and so cold that icicles form at the edges of my habit and keep striking my legs, and blood flows from the wounds. And I come to the gate, all covered with mud and cold and ice, and after I have knocked and called for a long time, a friar comes and asks: 'Who are you?' I answer: 'Brother Francis.' And he says: 'Go away. This is not a decent time to be going about. You can't come in.'

"And when I insist again, he replies: 'Go away. You're a simple and uneducated man. From now on, don't stay with us any more. We are so numerous and important that we don't need you.'

"But I still stand at the gate and say: 'For the love of God, let me come in tonight.' And he answers: 'I won't. Go to the Crosiers' Place and ask there!'

"I tell you that if I *kept patience* and was *not upset*— that is *true joy* and tested virtue and the salvation of my soul."[4]

It would almost seem from this story that St. Francis was a masochist—taking pleasure in his suffering. Even the theme of a homily he once gave in 1213 hints at the same:

> *Tanto è il bene ch'io aspetto*
> *ch'ogni pena m'è diletto.*

> So great the good I have in sight
> that every pain I count delight.[5]

And he wrote in *Admonition 5*: "But in this we can *glory*: in our *infirmities* and bearing daily the holy cross of our Lord Jesus Christ."[6]

But Francis is far from a masochist. Francis seems to have embraced this theme of joy in suffering from the Scriptures. We always speak of eight beatitudes. I always like to say that's because we don't particularly like the ninth beatitude: "Blessed are you when people revile you and persecute you and utter all kinds of evil against you falsely on my account. *Rejoice and be glad*, for your reward is great in heaven" [Matthew 5:11-12]. Jesus is telling us to be joyful in times of persecution of whatever sort. The apostles seem to have learned this lesson well: "After (the apostles) left the council, they rejoiced that they were considered worthy to suffer dishonor for the sake of the name" [Acts 5:41].

I was also surprised to pick up this theme in *The Brothers Karamazov* by Dostoevsky. One of the Karamazov brothers, Alyosha, was apprenticed to the elder monk Zosima and visited him daily. When Alyosha went to visit Zosima for the last time before his death, Zosima said to him, "Christ is with you. Do not abandon Him and He will not abandon you. You will know great sorrow and in that sorrow you will find happiness. Seek happiness through sorrow." [7]

Henri Nouwen seems to summarize almost all that is said above about hope in these words:

> The French author Simon Weil writes in her notebooks: *Waiting patiently in expectation is the foundation of the spiritual life.* These words express powerfully how absence and presence are never separated in the experience of God. The spiritual life is, first of all, a *patient waiting*, that is, *a waiting in suffering* during which the many experiences of unfulfillment remind us of God's absence. But this life is also a *waiting in expectation* which allows us to recognize the first signs of the coming of God *in the center of our pains.* Therefore, the mystery of God's presence can only be touched by a deep awareness of (God's) absence. It is in the center of our longing for the

absent God that we discover *(God's) footprints* and realize that our desire to love God is born out of the love with which (God) has touched us. It is in the *patient waiting* for the loved one that we discover how much (God) has filled our lives already.

In our *impatient culture* it has indeed become extremely difficult to see much salvation *in waiting*. But still the God who saves is not made by human hands. God transcends our psychological distinctions between already and not yet, between absence and presence, between leaving and returning. And so in a *patient waiting in expectation* we can slowly break away from our illusions and make our lives into an unending prayer.

Prayer, in a sense, is a *hopeful waiting* on God, which we do not have to do alone, but in community. The community can offer the protective boundaries in which our love for God can mature in a *watchful waiting*. In the community we can affirm that indeed our lives are *waiting lives*. There we can be *patient*, that is, we can let the *suffering of each day* slowly convert our illusions into the prayer of a contrite heart. . . . The Christian community is a *waiting community*, that is, a community which not only offers a sense of belonging, but also a sense of estrangement. In the Christian community we can say we are together, but we cannot fulfill each other. We can support each other but we should also keep reminding each other that our destiny is beyond our togetherness. In the Christian community we have to *support each other in waiting*, and that requires that we keep criticizing anyone who makes community into a safe shelter or a cozy clique, and keep stimulating each other to move on to unknown worlds.[8]

And when St. Francis prays for "firm hope," I suspect he had the following Scripture in mind: "We have this hope, a sure and steadfast anchor of the soul, a hope that enters the inner shrine behind the curtain, where Jesus, a forerunner on our behalf, has entered" [Hebrews 6:19-20]. The anchor is the symbol of hope. And it is the anchor of a ship that keeps it on an even keel when beset by storms, the anchor being a symbol of Jesus, our Anchor, who stabilizes us in the suffering and storms of our lives.

I had the opportunity in Rome to attend a live performance of *Forza Venite Gente*, a musical on the life of St. Francis. The scene which touched me most was when Francis was alone on the stage at the end of his life, surrounded by an ethereal mist. From behind him came a woman covered completely with a sheer cloth dancing her way to him, around him, finally inviting him into the dance. And when he joined her in the dance, they both disappeared. It was his dance with Sister Death.

Our entire life is a life of waiting to be united with our Anchor, Jesus Christ! And there are many instances of suffering that we all experience like an anchored ship in a storm. When a storm subsides, the anchor is pulled back into the ship so it can move on. When all the storms of our life subside, our Anchor Jesus Christ will draw each of us to himself. It will be our invitation to dance with Sister Death through the mist, through the veil into the arms of Jesus Christ. I look forward to this dance!

St. Paul urges us, "We also boast in our sufferings, knowing that suffering produces endurance, and endurance produces character; and character produces hope, and hope does not disappoint us" [Romans 5:3-5]. At the end of the same letter he says, "For whatever was written in former days was written for our instruction, so that by steadfastness and by the encouragement of the Scriptures we might have hope" [Romans 15:4].

At every celebration of Eucharist, after the *Our Father* the presider prays that we be delivered from all evil, sin, anxiety—in short, all suffering—as we *wait in joyful hope* for the coming of Jesus Christ. This stance of waiting in patience is the hope that ultimately invites us into the dance that leads into paradise.

To assist you in your meditation:

1. Like St. Francis, meditate on the Scripture readings or just the Gospel of the day, or on a text from the Bible. Some suggestions on this theme of hope are:

      Isaiah 30: 15, 18 in the New American Bible translation

      Matthew 5:11-12; 13:2

      Luke 6:22-23; 12:43

      Acts of the Apostles 5:41

      Romans 5:1-5; 8:24-25

      Ephesians 1:12;18

      Hebrews 6:19

      1 Peter 1:13; 3:15

2. Again, like St. Francis, meditate on some divine mystery. Gaze at the *Christus Patiens*—the suffering Christ—on any crucifix. His body twisted wretchedly as he literally hung there on the cross. What hope was his? Searching for further elements of hope, meditate on the Passion, the suffering Christ Jesus endured, being nailed to the cross, and on his death that resulted from such inhumane suffering.

3. St. Francis also meditated on meeting God/Jesus in some encounter of the day. What is your experience or encounter today with suffering or death? What was the unseen for you today that called you to "hang in there" and hope?

St. Francis inscribed this Tau cross on a parchment
given to Brother Leo on Mount LaVerna,
perhaps with the words of Pope Innocent III ringing in his ears
to become a champion of the Tau cross
for love of the One who died thereon for us.
The Tau cross and the Crucifix of San Damiano have become
recognizable symbols of solidarity for all Franciscans.

Love

Saint Francis prayed:
and give me   *et da me*
perfect charity   *caritade perfecta*

****

A reading from the *Legend of the Three Companions:*

People saw how the brothers rejoiced in the midst of trials and tribulation; how zealous they were in prayer . . . and *how they really loved one another.* Seeing all this, many became convinced the brothers were true disciples of Jesus Christ; and with remorse in their hearts they came to ask the brothers pardon for having previously injured and insulted them. The brothers forgave them gladly, saying: "God forgive you." Some men asked to be received as companions, and because the brothers were few, Francis had authorized all six of them to accept new recruits; and with these they all returned to St. Mary of the Angels. When they were all together, joy filled their hearts, and they no longer remembered past injuries.

They were constant in prayer and in working with their hands. . . . They rose at midnight and prayed with many sighs. *And each deeply loved the other and cared for him as a mother cares for a cherished only child. Charity burned so ardently in their hearts that it was easy to risk life itself, not only for love of Jesus Christ, but also for the soul and body of any one of the brothers.*

One day two of the brothers came upon a madman who started throwing stones at them; and when one saw a stone aimed at the other he intercepted it, wishing rather to receive the blow himself. Indeed, each was ready to give his life for the other, so *deeply rooted were they in mutual love.*

If by chance a brother let fall some word that might disturb another, his conscience bothered him so sharply that he could not rest until, prostrate on the ground, he had confessed his fault, asking that his brother's foot should be placed on his mouth. . . .

Once in Cyprus, in the presence of a nobleman of the place, it happened that a brother named Barbaro said something that disturbed another brother. Seeing this Barbaro took up some asses' dung from the road and started to eat it saying: "Let the mouth which said a hurtful word to a brother submit to this shameful punishment." On seeing this, the nobleman was so edified that he offered himself and all his goods to the friars to be used as they thought best.[1]

A reading from the *Legend of Perugia:*

The day on which Lady Jacoba prepared the cake for blessed Francis, he remembered Brother Bernard and said to his companions: "That cake would please Brother Bernard. Go and tell Brother Bernard to come here immediately." The brother left at once and brought Brother Bernard to him. He sat down at the foot of the bed and said: "Father, I beg you to bless me and to *give me some evidence of your affection. If you manifest it to me with a fatherly tenderness, I believe that the other brothers of the Order and God as well will love me more for it.*

Francis put his hand on his head and blessed him, saying: "Write down what I am going to say. Brother Bernard was the first brother the Lord gave me. He was the first one who put into practice and fulfilled the perfection of the Gospel to the letter by distributing all his goods to the poor. *For that and for many other merits, I am obliged to love him more than any other brother of the Order. I wish, therefore, and order that the General Minister, whoever he is, cherish and honor him as myself, that the provincial ministers and the brothers look upon him as taking my place.*" These words were a cause of great consolation to Brother Bernard and for all those who were present.[2]

****

In his *Prayer Before a Crucifix* St. Francis asks his "Most High, Glorious God" for the gift of "perfect charity." We shall speak of his chosen adjective shortly, but before I treat of the notion of love itself, let us take a look at who is the person who loves? And I would like to use Scripture to attempt a response to this question. In the First Letter of Paul to the Thessalonians, chapter 1, verse 23, we read: "May ... the God of peace preserve you whole and entire — *spirit, soul and body,* irreproachable . . ." In this verse of Scripture, Paul speaks of the human person as three dimensional. I would like to make some comments on each of these dimensions.

First, the physical, human body. The body makes demands on us. We must sleep it, wash it, feed it, empty it, clothe it, doctor it, etc. It grows sick, old, tired, reminding us of its limitations. Occasionally, it will embarrass us if we do not attend to it. The body can control us through addictions to food, drink, sex or drugs. The body holds memories. For example, what is my history of touch? Was I caressed as a baby/child or possibly abused? The body is, perhaps, the basis or foundation of much of our experience.

We read in the book of Genesis 1:31 that when God created humanity on the sixth day, God said: "It was very good!" And Richard Rohr remarks: "We are the only world religion that worships a God who took on a body!"[3] Franciscan Blessed John Duns Scotus speaks of the Incarnation of Jesus in terms of Christ being the primacy of God's creation. Moreover, St. Paul asks: "Do you not know that your body is a temple of the Holy Spirit within you, which you have from God?" [1 Corinthians 6:19]

Eric Doyle, OFM, wrote; "Carl Jung considered the Assumption to be the most important religious event since the Reformation.... being based on a belief stretching back for more than a thousand years.... Jung saw the definition as an event of great significance,"[4] the most extraordinary doctrine of the last 500 years perhaps because part of us is in the beyond. This is not found in Scripture but in the collective unconscious.

So the human body is good, and our God took on this human form as well. And the body of the Mother of Christ, Mary, has been assumed into heaven, putting the human body in a very precious light!

Christianity as a religion centers its worship on the body of Christ in the Eucharist—This is my body—Jesus' words spoken by every presider. And when the Eucharist is distributed, the person says: "The body of Christ," a very physical statement, not the "spirit" or "soul" of Christ. Moreover, the entire Eucharistic service is an expression of body language—we kneel, stand, sit, kiss, sign ourselves. The Franciscan patron of the Eucharist is St. Paschal Baylon whose last name has overtones to the Spanish *bailar* meaning to dance. He supposedly came from a family of dancers. Dancing expresses body talk.

There is the story of the bishop from Rome who was supervising the assembly of the Vatican Pavilion during the last World's Fair in New York. Michaelangelo's *Pietà* was the centerpiece of the exhibit. The Vatican bishop set up the pavilion so that the people had to pass through the chapel in front of the main altar to visit the *Pietà*. The bishops of New York were concerned with the set-up because they said the people outside waiting in line to get in would enter the pavilion in shorts, smoking, eating, drinking, etc., all of which would be most disrespectful before the Blessed Sacrament. The Vatican bishop responded, "It may be the only time in their lives that they'll be that close to Jesus Christ." And he left it as planned!

Turning our attention to the second dimension of the human person—the soul, let us take a look at what St. Bonaventure says of the human soul. When writing of the soul of the human person in chapter three of *The Journey of the Human Person Into God*,[5] St. Bonaventure treats of the faculties of memory, intellect and will. He wrote, "Here you can see God through yourself as through an image."[6] It is precisely in the human soul and through the use of its faculties that one can pick up an image of the Trinity, the God who dwells within us. Through the use of memory one picks up an image of God the Father who is Eternal; through the use of the intellect one picks up an image of God the Son who is Truth; through the use of the will one picks up an image of God the Spirit who is the Highest Good. And deciding to seek for the Highest Good is to seek for love, the greatest gift of all.

In another meditation on *The Five Feasts of the Child Jesus*, when St. Bonaventure writes about the feast of the Epiphany, he speaks of the three Magi as the three powers of the soul that constantly go in search of the Child as did the Magi, especially when life's challenges need the support of the divine presence.

And in the Prologue to his *Tree of Life* which are meditations on the life of Jesus, Bonaventure mentions other faculties of the soul, namely, imagination and affectivity. He writes, " Imagination aids understanding [intellect]."[7] Then Bonaventure invites the reader to "feel" what Christ felt; "an affection and feeling of this kind is merited to be experienced in a vital way by the one who . . . contemplates."[8]

Finally, some comments on the third dimension of the human person, the spirit. You would have noticed that the word spirit was written in lower case letters because Scripture is speaking of the spirit of the human person, not the Holy Spirit. "We must remember," writes Watchman Nee, "that . . . it is the human spirit where God dwells, where (God's) Spirit mingles with our spirit."[9] St. Paul writes, "It is that very Spirit bearing witness within our spirit that we are children of God" [Romans 8:16]. Carroll Stuhlmueller writes:

> One of the ways by which we follow Jesus into his mysterious life with the Father and the Spirit, is to allow our own spirit come to rest in the deepest part of ourselves. Here is where the temple of God is constructed; here is the Holy of Holies of that temple, here resides the Ark of the Covenant, containing

the tablets of the law. Here is where we hear God's word. . . . Before this Holy of Holies, the seraphim continually call out: "Holy, holy, holy is the Lord of hosts—*Qadosh! Qadosh! Qadosh! Yahwek seb'aoth!* Holy—in Hebrew *qadosh*—means separation, overwhelming distance, awesome transcendence, as fearful as approaching the sun, as murky and black as the bottom of the ocean. Yet, this same God speaks with us and calls us "friend!" We can approach this God—we can fly into the sun and sink to the ocean depths. The more personal is God's embrace, the more profound is our ecstasy of Love.

When we settle into the depths of ourselves, we hear God speak our name. . . . We must let our spirit come to rest at the depths of ourselves, so that we can hear that name, that word of ourselves spoken again, with the pure strong accents of God's voice.[10]

In order for us to experience such an intimacy with our God, we must open ourselves to deep union with God. We can choose to do this on our own, and Evagrius of Pontus would call this *praktikos*[11] in Greek, a spiritual discipline that comes from a regular life of prayer. It is the ordinary, normal path we are invited to take. It's similar to what happens in nature. Jesus said: "Very truly I tell you, unless a grain of wheat falls into the earth and dies, it remains just a single grain; but if it dies, it bears much fruit" [John 12:24].

I remember the first time I planted a garden with my Father in our backyard in Brooklyn. I was very young, and my Dad asked me to plant some seeds. After professing my ignorance, he instructed me step by step. First, dig a hole, and then place the seeds in the earth. I dug the hole and put the seeds into it, but I would not cover them. When Dad came back to me to ask why I did not cover them, I told him it reminded me too much of a funeral. Whenever I attended a relative's burial as a child, they would lower the coffin and proceed to cover it with the earth. It was such a sad time. And

I felt sad burying the seeds. Then my Dad told me that the seeds would be quite content if I covered them with the soft earth. The temperature, nutrients and watering would all work on the seeds, inviting them to break open and send forth shoots to grow into plants to give us tomatoes, peppers or squash. "Unless a kernel of wheat falls to the ground and dies, it remains only a single seed. But if it dies, it produces . . ." So very natural!

Clare seems to have known this, for we read in the papal bull for her canonization: "Moreover, since in the austerity of her cloistered solitude, *she broke the alabaster jar* of her body with her severity, the whole church *was thoroughly imbued* with the aroma of her sanctity."[12] She opened her spirit to her Beloved.

However, if we do not work at *praktikos* in our spiritual lives so as to open ourselves to God, God sometimes breaks us open. And such an experience can be very painful. Just take the example of a woman religious who is CEO in one of her congregation's hospitals. She rises at 5:00 am, showers, dresses, has breakfast, drives several miles and is at her desk by 7:00 am. She spends an hour planning her entire day of meetings, conferences, consultations, committees, etc. She leaves the hospital by 7:00 pm, is at home by 8:00, eats, relaxes a bit and then retires by 10:00 pm. There has been little or no time alone with God. But she justifies this as ministry for the congregation with a substantial salary, etc. And one day, after living this way for a long time, she has a stroke and finds herself in the same hospital, this time in a bed. She will survive, but with some lengthy rehabilitation. And she has time to evaluate the direction of her life up to now. She may see that her pressured daily schedule left little time for God. She feels "broken," finds herself thinking of her relationship with God and how precious little time she has spent with her Beloved. In a sense we can say that God broke her open to grab her attention.

Being broken open by God seems to have been the experience of Francis in his conversion process. He abhorred lepers; God brought him one to embrace. He sought fame through knighthood;

God taught him to glory in the cross! It would seem that God had to break Francis open, and this hurt broke through his skin in the form of the stigmata—the wounds of Jesus—so that divinity could unite and dwell with his spirit!

Having considered the three dimensional composition of the human person from the First Letter to the Thessalonians 5:23, it would seem that Luke 1:46 evokes an awareness of the same tripartite dimensions of the human person. In this verse, the pregnant Mary is with her cousin Elizabeth. She is with child—her body is making this child grow. As Damien Isabell, OFM, once remarked in the chapel of the Porziuncola in Assisi before the icon of the Annunciation: "Mary's 'yes' to God freed God of invisibility!" But she was with child before she was with Joseph, and this put her in jeopardy with Hebrew law. Nevertheless, she did not let this problem overwhelm her. Regarding her child, all Mary's thoughts, memories, desires, emotions and fantasies—that is, every dimension of her soul—magnified her God. Her soul made God great, not her problem. And because of such inner and outer exuberance, her spirit rejoiced in this pregnancy that was making the God she always worshipped intimately present in her and physically to the entire world. So according to Scripture, this is the make-up of the human person who loves.

Now let us look at what love means. This is not easy, for love has as many definitions as there are persons who love. Nevertheless, I offer what love has come to mean to me as I've attempted walk in love in my own life.

If I could sum up what a process of love would look like, it would be a commitment to which I say "yes," a commitment that demands work.

St. Paul gives us an understanding of love in his famous passage of 1 Corinthians 13. It would be such an understanding of love to which I would commit myself, to which I say "yes" with my entire being. But trying to live just one line of that famous passage doesn't just happen. Such a love in not spontaneous! It costs me every time I try to be patient or kind or altruistically centered. At times, the cost is paid in some form of pain. And just doing it demands much energy and investment on my part. And this is why I believe that one must work at a love relationship for love to stay alive and flourish.

Returning to the stories about the early brothers, their love for one another was something that was fostered, cherished and worked at daily. And Francis put his own personal stamp on how the brothers were to love. A good number of the early friars who came to join Francis could neither read nor write. So Francis could not tell them to check out passages in the Gospels that teach them about love. But when he walked through Assisi with the brothers and came upon a mother carrying a child, he would stop them, point at the mother and child saying: "If a mother loves and cares for her child in the flesh, a friar should certainly love and care for his spiritual brother all the more tenderly."[13] Two important dimensions emerge from his own personal stamp on love. First, Francis uses motherly love as the paradigm for the friars. This is a very nurturing type of love. And secondly, it is a love that is delicate, sensitive, warm—in a word, tender. He calls the brothers to a tender love—a love that is affectionate, gentle, compassionate.

And in his *Letter to a Certain Minister,* Francis calls us to an almost heroic type of love, a love that literally goes beyond the seventy-times-seven Jesus urges on Peter:

> I should like you to prove that you love God and me, his servant and yours, in the following way. There should be no friar in the whole world who has fallen into sin, no matter how far he has fallen, who will ever fail to find your forgiveness for the asking, if he will only look into your eyes. And if he does not ask forgiveness, you should ask him if he wants it. And should he appear before

you again a thousand times, you should *love him more than you love me*, so that you may draw him to God; you should always have pity on such friars. Tell the guardians, too, that this is your policy.[14]

In his prayer Francis prays for "perfect love." It would seem that he has the First Letter of St. John in mind: "There is no fear in love, but perfect love casts out fear" [4:18]. As Francis became more intimate with God in prayer, this intimacy gradually eradicated fears in him. This is an ongoing process, taking time and work to accomplish. And though his love may not have been "perfect"—a word usually attributed to God—nevertheless, the deeper the intimacy, the more mature the love. And maturity in love brings a confidence that would eradicate fear.

Perhaps the word "balance" instead of perfection, could help us here. Richard Rohr, OFM, remarked that since the human person who loves is composed of body, soul and spirit, then when all three dimensions are in a balance, it is then that we can be called biblical persons of the heart.[15] And it is the heart which is the symbol of love! Balance, then, does not equate with perfection, but it does indicate a type of equilibrium, stability or steadiness that gives us a sense of spiritual poise.

Faith, hope and love are called theological virtues. *Theos* is the Greek word for God. So these three are God-virtues. We are familiar with 1 John 4:16 which reads: "God is love." If God is love and these three virtues—faith, hope, love—are *Theos* virtues, then we can say that God is faith, God is hope. It is God in us who believes, hopes, loves. Eric Doyle, OFM, writes:

> One way of describing the mystery within us is to say that we are a unity of matter and spirit. In this unity is located the divine spark which is continually striving to burst into the flame of love without limits. But it needs our free cooperation. Even the slightest effort to do so bears fruit at once in a growth of awareness of other beings.[16]

And Carroll Stuhlmueller says, "At the depths of our selves is a perception, an intuition, a *divine spark*."[17] These "divine sparks" of faith, hope and love are signs of God's presence within us. They are gifts given us at baptism. We can never lose them, but we can refuse to use them. But every time we believe, hope or love, we ignite this divine spark into the flame of God's holy presence. Bonaventure says, "It is God alone who is this fire, and God's *furnace is in Jerusalem*. And it is Christ who starts the fire with the white flame of his most intense passion."[18]

Let me conclude these reflections with a series of experiences I had with my Father. I remember being at table eating in my Mother's kitchen and my Father was on the phone with my niece Jessica. At the end of the conversation with this ten-year-old, my Father said, "OK, Jessica, Grandpa has to go. I love you!" As he hung up the phone, I remember thinking, "He never told me that!"

When my Father was in the last months of his life, dementia began to take hold of him. And we had to care for him day and night. We had a woman who came in during the day while my brother and I worked. But she could not come in during Holy Week that year.

So I was with my Dad day and night. Since he could not shower alone anymore, we had to help him with this. I remember on Holy Thursday putting on a pair of walking shorts and getting him into the shower. I was begrudgingly doing this, thinking of Christians throughout the world gathering together that day to begin the Sacred Triduum. And here I was in my shorts trying to shower a man who didn't want a shower! "The water's too hot!" he complained. "The soap burns my eyes!" The more he complained, the angrier I became. I remember kneeling before Dad washing his feet, and I heard the words inside myself, "THIS IS MY BODY!" It was a Eucharistic moment I'll never forget. The shower water drenched me, but I had tears in my eyes.

Dimentia overtook Dad almost completely. When I went to see him at Cabrini Nursing Home right before he died, I walked into the room, and when my Father saw me, he called me by my baptismal name. I knew he knew who I was; it was a lucid moment. I went right up to his face and said, "Dad, I love you!" He looked at me quizzically and said, "But I have always loved you!"

St. Bonaventure writes: "And such is the power of your love, O soul, that, as Bernard writes, 'You live more truly where you love than where you breathe.' This, dearest soul, is the kingdom of God within us."[19]

To assist you in your meditation:

1. Like St. Francis, meditate on the Scripture readings or just the Gospel of the day, or on a text from the Bible. Some suggestions are on this theme of love are:

Matthew 5:43-48

Mark 12:28-34

Luke 1:46; 7:36-50

John 12:24

Romans 8:16

1 Thessalonians 1:3; 5:23

1 Corinthians 6: 19; 13

1 John 4:7-21.

2. Again, like St. Francis, meditate on some divine mystery. There is a red Tau[20] painted on the window frame in the Magdalen

chapel at Fonte Colombo, which "drawing dates back to St. Francis himself."[21] St. Francis was fond of the Tau cross, using it to sign his letters, marking doors and walls of cells, and for healing.[22] Innocent III urged all who attended the Fourth Lateran Council to "be champions of the Tau and of the cross!"[23] Meditate on the mystery of the cross as an expression of God's love for us. How is the cross—the instrument of death—the symbol of God's love for us?

3. St. Francis also meditated on meeting God/Jesus in some encounter of the day. What is your experience or encounter today with the cross that Christ Jesus invites each of us to take up, to embrace in love?

This crucifix, painted by Alberto Sozio in 1187,
hangs in the Cathedral of Spoleto.
It depicts Mary clearly as the one whose "yes" to God's will
freed God from invisibility by the birth of her Son.
The figure of Jesus closely resembles the same figure
on the Crucifix of San Damiano,
the artist and dating of which remain unknown.

The Will of God

Saint Francis prayed:

so that I may carry out	*che faça*
Your holy and true	*lo tuo santo et verace*
command.	*commandamento.*

****

A reading from *The Little Flowers of St. Francis:*

Once St. Francis was traveling in Tuscany with Brother Masseo . . . walking along a road with Brother Masseo going a bit ahead of St. Francis. But when they came to a crossroads where three roads met, where they could go to Siena or Florence or Arezzo, Brother Masseo said: "Father Francis, *which road should we take?*" St. Francis replied: "We will take the road God wants us to take." Brother Masseo said: *"How will we be able to know God's will?"* St. Francis answered: "By the sign I will show you. Now under the merit of holy obedience I command you to twirl around in this crossroads, right where you are standing, just as children do, and not to stop turning until I tell you."

So Brother Masseo obediently began to turn around, and he twirled around so long that he fell down several times from dizziness in his head, which usually results from such turning. But as St. Francis did not tell him to stop, and he wanted to obey faithfully, he got up again and resumed his gyrations.

Finally, after he had been twirling around bravely for a long time, St. Francis said: "Stand still! Don't move!" And Brother Masseo stood still. And St. Francis asked him: "What direction are you facing?"

"Toward Siena," replied Brother Masseo.

"That's the road God wants us to take," said St. Francis.[1]

"If this were the only account of Franciscan discernment, it probably would be best that we simply ignore the account and not speak of a Franciscan process of discernment," wrote Anthony Carrozzo.[2] But we do have a more substantial resource in the following account.

A reading from *The Little Flowers of St. Francis*:

Narrator: The *humble servant* of Christ, St. Francis, at the beginning of his conversion was *placed in a great agony of doubt* as to what he should do: whether to give himself only to continual prayer or to preach sometimes. He wanted very much to know which of these would please Jesus Christ the most. And as the humility that was in him did not allow him to trust in himself or in his own prayers, he humbly *turned to others* in order to know God's will in this matter. So he called Brother Masseo and said to him:

Francis: Dear Brother, go to Sister Clare and tell her on my behalf to pray devoutly to God with one of her companions that God may show me what is best: either that I preach sometimes or that I devote myself only to prayer. And then go to Brother Sylvester, who is staying on Mount Subasio, and tell him the same thing.

Narrator: Brother Sylvester was so devout and holy that God immediately granted or revealed to him whatever he asked in prayer, and St. Francis was devoted to him and had great faith in him. Brother Masseo went, and as St. Francis had ordered him, gave the message first to Sister Clare and then to Brother Sylvester.

Sylvester immediately set himself to praying and quickly had God's answer. And he went out at once to Brother Masseo and said:
Sylvester: God says you are to tell Brother Francis this: that God has not called him to this state only on his own account, but that he may reap a harvest of souls and that many may be saved through him.

Narrator: After this Brother Masseo went back to Sister Clare to know what she had received from God. And she answered:

Clare: Both I and my companion had the very same answer from God as Brother Sylvester.

Narrator: Brother Masseo returned to St. Francis. And the Saint received him with great charity. He *washed his feet and prepared a meal for him.* And after he had eaten, St. Francis called Brother Masseo into the woods. And there he knelt down before Brother Masseo, and baring his head and crossing his arms, St. Francis asked him:

Francis: *What does my Lord Jesus Christ order me to do?*

Masseo: God answered both Brother Sylvester and Sister Clare and her companion and revealed that: "God wants you to go about the world preaching, because God did not call you for yourself alone but also for the salvation of others."

Narrator: As soon as St. Francis heard this answer and thereby knew the will of Christ, he got to his feet, all aflame with divine power, said to Brother Masseo with great fervor:

Francis: So let's go—in the name of the Lord![3]

****

When it comes down to trying to figure out the will of God in our lives, I would like to suggest that God's will is already known—namely—that we be Gospel people, that we incarnate the Word of God in our lives. What we are seeking, I would submit, is what *way* or *path* we are to take in our lives as Gospel people.

I live in a friary that is directly north of New York City. When I have to go to our provincial friary in the heart of Manhattan, I have a choice of three different highways. The destination is the same, the road I choose to get there can vary. So I don't get out of my car and twirl around in the middle of the road seeking a direction. I need to determine, to consider, to discern the best road depending on the time of day, the amount of traffic and the distance. When it comes down to a choice of a way, a path or a road in life, I think we are dealing with discernment.

In his first biography of St. Francis, Thomas of Celano wrote that Francis "longed to know what might be more acceptable to the eternal King concerning himself or in himself or what might happen. Most carefully he himself sought out and most piously longed to know *in what manner, by what way,* by what desire he might cling perfectly to God according to the good pleasure of God's will."[4]

In a work once attributed to St. Bonaventure, he defines discernment as "a foresighted consideration of the things that need to be done."[5] Since Vatican II, discernment has become a "buzz" word in the spiritual life. And this is healthy because people are taking more seriously their relationship with God as they try to walk by "following the footsteps of our Lord Jesus Christ."[6]

In its first meaning, discernment is the process by which one distinguishes evil from good.[7] However, there are times in our lives when we are not faced with a choice between good or evil. Choices are sometimes morally neutral, and sometimes one faces a choice between two goods. More about this later.

Anthony Carrozzo, OFM, was one of the first Franciscans to write about the possibility of a Franciscan process of discernment. In his article already cited (see endnote 2), he makes use of the story about Francis' quandary as to whether he should continue preaching or devote himself to prayer, in order to tease out steps and qualities that might accompany such a discernment process. I have made use of this process with individuals in spiritual direction several times.[8] I have divided this process into three steps and five qualities that should accompany a Franciscan process of personal discernment. I will examine these steps and qualities and follow up with an example.

THREE STEPS

STEP 1

The account begins: "The *humble servant* of Christ, St. Francis, at the beginning of his conversion . . ." At the outset, Francis is called *humble*. If a person enters into a process of Franciscan discernment, then, like Francis, one must enter into that process in humility. Being humble does not mean that one becomes a doormat for people to trample. That's humiliation! A humble person is a person of the truth. The word humble comes from the Latin *humus*, meaning "the earth."

I had a hard time connecting the two together until I realized that if one plants an orange seed, then Mother Earth gives an orange tree. She doesn't give a peach tree. The earth does not lie! "Humility involves, most basically, the awareness, that deep down, we are not of our own making," writes Zachary Hayes.[9] We recognize that our earthy nature is drawn from the *humus*. We are not our own—this is the deepest truth. Hayes continues: "What is an appropriate response to this deep truth of our being? . . . St. Francis comes to speak of all creatures as 'brothers and sisters'. . . . Humility is the first step in the journey."[10]

Francis is called a "humble *servant.*" Calling Francis a servant evokes the incident in chapter 13 of the Gospel of John where Jesus washes the feet of his disciples. In his *Office of the Passion* St. Francis composed an antiphon which he prayed fourteen times each day to remind him of this attitude of service:

The antiphon concludes with a recall of a Gospel scene of great significance for Francis, namely the washing of the disciples' feet by Jesus, who at the end of this action, says to them: "Do you know what I have done for you? You call me *Teacher* and *Lord*, and rightly so, for indeed I am. If I, therefore, the *Lord and Teacher*, have washed your feet, you ought to wash one another's feet. I have given you an example so that as I have done for you, you should also do" [John 13:12-15] In giving to Christ the title *Lord and Teacher*, the conclusion of the antiphon well situates the Hero of the geste as the Teacher of whom Francis is an attentive disciple and as the Lord who has come "not to be served but to serve and give his life as a ransom." [Matthew 20:28]. This attitude of service is really what Francis' psalms are all about.[11]

So a prerequisite for initiating a Franciscan process of personal discernment would necessitate a consideration of one being a "humble servant."

STEP 2

"St. Francis, at the beginning of his conversion, was *placed in a great agony of doubt* as to what he should do: whether to give himself only to continual prayer or to preach sometimes." As was already mentioned before, discernment in St. Francis' life was dealing with a choice between two goods:

good #1) to continue an itinerant life of preaching;
good #2) to focus completely on a life of prayer.

My suspicion about a possible backdrop to this story might be due to the fact that Clare was already living a contemplative life with her sisters at San Damiano. Francis himself from his very early years spent time in solitude whenever he could. Dacian Bluma,

OFM, claims that "Francis spent up to half of his converted life in solitude." The active life on the road was a sharp contrast to what he experienced when he was in solitude or whenever he visited with Clare. He loved preaching to the people, but equally enjoyed his times of solitude. And having these contrasting experiences churning around inside himself is what may have raised the doubt in him about his lifestyle accompanied by a struggle or agony about what "would please Jesus Christ the most."

So a second prerequisite for a Franciscan process of personal discernment would be "agony of doubt" concerning a choice between two goods in one's life—although the choice could concern three or more goods.

STEP 3

"And as the humility that was in him did not allow him to trust in himself or in his own prayers, he humbly turned to others in order to know God's will in this matter."

Carrozzo notes that "two very important Franciscan values are expressed here:

> a. the *Spirit speaks through others*—the incarnational value;
> b. this process of discernment is based on *personal poverty*—that is, the discerner needs to move towards others in order to discover where it is that God is drawing the discerner."[13]

It is obvious here that St. Francis believed that the Spirit would speak through the people he chose to discern with him. The operative word here is "believe," for Francis was ready to risk all on the faith premise that God's direction for him would be revealed to others. This basic belief is bolstered by St. Francis' personal poverty, his willingness to depend on God for everything that pertained to his life. The Scripture, "do not worry about your life," [Matthew 6:25] supports Francis' stance especially because the choice before him concerns two goods; so either way, he cannot lose!

Carrozzo again: "Francis did not turn to just anyone for the help he sought. Rather, he uses *three criteri*a in choosing these mediators of the Spirit:

> a. the person chosen must be *conversant with God*; that is, the person must be filledwith the Spirit of God through a life of *prayer*;
> b. the discerner must be very devoted to the person who is chosen . . . toward whom the discerner has a *deep affection and intimate relationship*;
> c. the discerner has *faith in the person* chosen so that at the end of the process one cannot say the persons chosen did not know what they were talking about."[14]

Each of us has a variety of good friends in our lives. However, when it comes to choosing a "mediator of the Spirit," it is clear that we would have to choose people to discern with us who themselves have a prayerful relationship with God. If one of our good friends does not value prayer, then such a person would not meet the criterion of being "conversant with God."

Moreover, we are invited to choose persons to whom we are "very devoted." This could include good friends, a spiritual director, a spouse, a brother or sister religious, one's pastor. Francis chose Sylvester and Clare, persons he cherished but did not necessarily spend a lot of time with them. In fact, he, at times, ignored Clare's invitations to visit her.

And the third criterion above challenges us to invest our faith in the persons we choose, risking all so that God's direction for our life would be made manifest.

In short, the three steps above can be summarized:

1.   The discerner must be a humble servant;
2.   The discerner must be in agony of doubt
        between two goods;
3.   The discerner turns towards others for
        prayerful help.

FIVE QUALITIES

As Carrozzo continues his analysis of the story, his commentary seems to tease out what I call five qualities that should accompany a Franciscan process of personal discernment. A brief consideration of each of them would be a good gauge that the discerner is moving in this process in a manner akin to Francis and his discernment.

1. Detachment

"Brother Masseo returned to St. Francis. And the Saint received him with great charity. He washed his feet and prepared a meal for him." More than likely, Francis and Masseo were at St. Mary of the Angels when this episode began. To walk from there to the San Damiano Monastery to see Clare would have taken a good hour. Then to go from the monastery to Mount Subasio where Sylvester was would have taken up to two more hours. Conservatively speaking, the round trip would have been about six hours long, a solid day of walking straight up, then down. And Masseo would have been understandably tired from the trek. So Francis, in a spirit of John 13, washed his feet. Humanly speaking, this would have felt quite good after such a long walk. The story continues, noting that St. Francis prepared a meal for him. We don't read about Francis cooking too frequently in the sources, but it was a very fraternal action for Francis to perform. I think that if I were in Francis' shoes, I'd want an answer from Masseo as soon as he returned to St. Mary of the Angels. But since Francis is dealing with two goods, he remains detached and waits until Masseo has eaten, because no matter the outcome, God blesses him with either choice.

2. Obedient trust

"And after he had eaten, St. Francis called Brother Masseo into the woods. And there he knelt down before Brother Masseo, and baring his head and crossing his arms, St. Francis asked him: 'What does my Lord Jesus Christ order me to do?' " It is fascinating that St. Francis did not ask Masseo what Clare or Sylvester said or concluded in their prayer for him. No. Because he believed that the Spirit of God speaks through prayerful persons, he asked what Jesus wants him to do, ready to hear with confidence—obedient trust—the result of their prayer.

3. Prayer

"It is important to note," writes Carrozzo, "that, while Masseo was going to Sylvester and Clare, Francis remained at prayer, praying not only for himself, but for the messenger and for those he chose to discern with him."[15] This is solid prayer support for the discernment and discerners. Perhaps Francis prayed this *Prayer Before a Crucifix* for God to enlighten the darkness of his heart.

4. Openness to the Spirit

One time when Brother Leo came to St. Francis for advice, the Saint gave him a response that Carrozzo calls "the Gospel of Franciscan Freedom."[16] St. Francis gave Leo a piece of parchment in his own handwriting with these words: "In whatever way you think you will best please our Lord God and to follow in his footsteps and in poverty, do this with God's blessing and with my obedience."[17] St. Francis leaves Leo completely free to respond to the Spirit in whatever way he thinks the Spirit is leading him. So, too, St. Francis himself walks in the freedom of the Spirit's lead in this story discerning his future.

5. Franciscan Initiative

At the end of the discernment, Francis says to Masseo: "So let's go—in the name of the Lord." It's clear to Francis what God asked of him, so poor Masseo who just returned from a full day of walking is on the move again with the Saint.

I already mentioned that I have been able to make use of this Franciscan process of personal discernment in spiritual direction. Let me share just one example.

A Franciscan Sister named Maryellen, who allows me to share this example, had been in spiritual direction with me for a long time. She was the novice director of her congregation. Her congregation sponsored a few hospitals, and one of them offered Maryellen a position for which she was well qualified with a lucrative salary attached. And the community could have made good use of the income.

I knew Maryellen to be a humble servant from the many months of spiritual dialogue together. She enjoyed her work in formation as novice director. And one of the other loves of her life was the health-care ministry. She was literally in agony of doubt with regard to these two goods set before her. I explained the process outlined above and she agreed to try it.

She immediately chose several other persons to discern with her. In addition to a sister-friend, she chose the leader of the community and the finance director. She met with each of them, outlined the two possibilities for ministry, and gave them several weeks to pray over these choices. At the end of these weeks, she made an appointment for all to see me.

When all parties involved in the discernment process arrived, we went into the chapel and sat in a circle. I began with prayer, and after a while, I invited each of them to share their discernment with

Maryellen. Each person spoke from her own prayer experience, at times backing up her words with passages from Scripture. And each woman, including the finance director, shared her discernment that Maryellen should remain as novice director and forego the hospital offer.

There was a spirit of detachment not only in Maryellen but also in the sisters who discerned with her, especially the finance director. Although Maryellen felt that health-care ministry was one of her gifts, she confidently heard her sisters' discernment in a spirit of obedient trust. Both Maryellen and her sisters spent many weeks in prayer concerning these two offers. And her openness to the Spirit was evident from the peace that was felt in Maryellen herself and the sisters with her. She immediately resumed her work in formation.

In closing, I would like to make a comment on feelings of resistance. While detachment and obedient trust are two important qualities of this discernment process, resistance to what God wants is experienced at times. We know from Jesus' life that he experienced resistance to what God wanted of him. I am referring to the incident in the garden of Gethsemani, his agony over the impending crucifixion and his prayer: "My Father, if it is possible, let this cup pass from me" [Matthew 26:39]. Perhaps he already witnessed crucifixions by the Romans. There was resistance in Jesus regarding his Father's will for him, a resistance that was real, normal and healthy. But at times, resistance can also be somewhat selfish. Let me explain by example.

In 1976 I received a phone call from the director of formation of my Franciscan province to scout out possibilities to move our postulant house to New York while another friar would scout out Boston. Shortly thereafter, a second phone call came asking: Would I be the director of the postulant house? I immediately felt resistance inside myself. I told him I would pray about it. My resistance arose from the possibility that I would have to leave structures I knew very well—my job at All Hallows Institute and the network of the New York archdiocese, not to mention leaving New York City itself.

I went to see my spiritual director, at that time a priest of the archdiocese. I thought he'd certainly favor my remaining in New York. In that session, he told me: "Like Abraham, pack your bags!" From a retreat I called a very good friend at the time and shared my dilemma with him, and he responded, "You'd make a fine formation director!" So, despite my inner, and selfish, resistance, I called the director of formation to accept the job.

I went to the formation board meeting that was held in Massachusetts to give my report on New York as a possible site while another brother reported on Boston. I felt the cards were stacked against me. After the members of the board heard our reports, they stood up to leave. I interrupted them as they got up and asked where they were going. They said they had to go to another room to vote. Since I was not officially appointed to formation work at that time, I could not participate in the decision. Needless to say, my anxiety grew stronger. When they came back to the room, to my happy surprise, they chose New York for the new formation unit.

To assist you in your meditation:

1. Like St. Francis, meditate on the Scripture readings or just the Gospel of the day, or on a text from the Bible. Some suggestions are on this theme of God's will are:

> Mark 3:31-35

> Luke 1:26-38; 2:19.

2. Again, like St. Francis, meditate on some divine mystery. Mary, the Mother of Jesus, stood beneath her son's cross. She carried out the will of God perfectly when she gave her *fiat*—her

"yes" — to the Archangel Gabriel. Meditate on this mystery of the Annunciation and Mary's "yes" to God's will for her which freed God of invisibility.

3. St. Francis also meditated on meeting God/Jesus in some encounter of the day. What is your experience or encounter today walking in the heart of God's will for you?

Conclusion

What I have written in each of these meditations is the fruit of my own personal meditation on the salient elements found in St. Francis' *Prayer Before a Crucifix*. As Francis meditated before any cross or crucifix, this was the prayer that welled up in his heart and flowed from his lips.

As I sang, recited or meditated on his words over the years, the wisdom and insights of other spiritual giants helped me unwrap more of the meaning of St. Francis' major themes—light, faith, hope, love and the will of God. I was then able to integrate these pearls of wisdom into my own thoughts and feelings during frequent meditative attempts to plumb their meaning.

In a sense, I share the journey of my own heart in these reflections in the hope that they would somehow become a springboard for you, the reader, to discover your own pearls of wisdom as you ponder this pithy and precious prayer of Francis of Assisi.

I close with the words of St. Francis' theologian, St. Bonaventure of Bagnoregio:

I ask, therefore,
that you give more attention
to the intent of the writer
than to the work itself,
more to the things said than to the uncultivated language,
more to the truth than to attractiveness,
more to the stimulation of affect than to intellectual enrichment.
So that this might happen, it is important
that you not run through these reflections in a hurry,
but that you take your time and ruminate over them slowly.[1]

ENDNOTES

Introduction

1 "Divine Praise and Meditation according to the Teaching and Example of St. Francis of Assisi,"Octavian Schmucki OFM Cap in *Greyfriars Review*, Vol. 4, No. 1, (The Franciscan Institute: St. Bonaventure, NY, 1990), p. 63, LMj IV:3, italics mine.

2 This text is in Francis' language spoken in Umbria. From *Opuscula Sancti Patris Francisci Assisiensis*, Caietanus Esser OFM (Collegii S. Bonaventurae Ad Claras Aquas: Grottaferrata, Roma, 1978), p. 224, author's translation.

3 Notes from a lecture delivered by Laurent Gallant OFM during *The Assisi Experience*, 1990.

4 "Divine Praise and Meditation according to the Teaching and Example of St. Francis of Assisi," op. cit., p. 62. Ibid. p. 67. Ibid. pp. 69-70.

5 Ibid., p. 67.

6 Ibid., pp. 69-70.

Light

1 *St. Francis of Assisi, Omnibus of Sources*, edited by Marion A. Habig, OFM, (Chicago, IL: Franciscan Herald Press, 1983), *The Little Flowers of St. Francis*, 15, pp. 1332-33, italics mine.

2 *Clare of Assisi: Early Documents*, edited and translated by Regis Armstrong, OFM Cap (New York: Franciscan Institute Publications, 1993), *Legend of St. Clare*, 2-3, p. 254, italics mine.

3 Ibid., *Bull of Canonization* 2-4, pp. 238-240, italics mine.

4 *St. Francis and the Song of Brotherhood and Sisterhood*, Eric Doyle OFM (New York: Franciscan Institute Publications,(1997), p. 86, italics mine.

5 *Clare, A Light in the Garden*, Murray Bodo OFM (Cincinnati: St. Anthony Messenger Press, 1992), p. 6, italics mine.

6 *The Little Flowers of St. Clare*, Piero Bargellini, translated by Edmund O'Gorman OFM Conv (Assisi: Edizioni Porziuncola, 1988), p. 59, italics mine.

7 *Workbook for Franciscan Studies*, Damien Isabell OFM (Chicago: Franciscan Herald Press, 1979), p. 88, translation of David Temple OFM.

8 *The Little Flowers of St. Clare*, op.cit., p. 83, italics mine.

9 Ibid., p. 84, italics mine.

10 Ibid., pp. 84-85, italics mine.

11 *Clare of Assisi: Early Documents*, op.cit., *Testament*, 24, p. 58, italics mine.

12 Ibid., *Form of Life of Clare of Assisi*, 9:4, p. 75, parenthesis mine.
13 *Clare, A Light in the Garden*, op.cit., pp. 17-18.
14 See *The Journey into God: A Forty-Day Retreat with Bonaventure, Francis and Clare*, Josef Raischl, SFO, and André Cirino, OFM (Cincinnati: St. Anthony Messenger Press, 2002), p. 352.

Faith

1 *St. Francis of Assisi, Omnibus of Sources*, op.cit., *Mirror of Perfection*, 85, p. 1218, italics mine.
2 Ibid. *The Little Flowers of St. Francis*, 2, pp. 1302-04; *Legend of the Three Companions*, 28-29, pp. 917-18.

Hope

1 *St. Francis of Assisi, Omnibus of Sources*, op.cit., *The Little Flowers of St. Francis*, 20, pp. 1346-47, italics mine.
2 *Biblical Meditations for Lent*, Carroll Stuhlmueller, CP (New York: Paulist Press, 1978) p. 138.
3 For further reading on meaningful suffering, see: "Beyond Surviving: Brother Cancer" in *America*, Robert Stewart, OFM (8 November 1997) pp. 27-29.
4 *St. Francis of Assisi, Omnibus of Sources*, op.cit., p.1501-02, adapted, italics mine.
5 *Francis of Assisi*, Arnaldo Fortini, translated by Helen Moak (New York: Crossroad, 1985) p. 550.
6 *Francis and Clare*, R. Armstrong, OFM Cap, and Ignatius Brady, OFM, (New York: Paulist Press, 1982), p. 29, italics mine.
7 *The Brothers Karamazov*, Fyodor Dostoevsky (Bantam Classics: New York, 1981), p. 89, italics mine.
8 From a cassette tape: *The Lonely Search for God*, Henri Nouwen (Notre Dame, Indiana: Ave Maria Press, 1990), Tape 2, adapted and italics mine.

Love

1 *St. Francis of Assisi, Omnibus of Sources*, op.cit., 41-43, pp. 929-931, italics mine.
2 Ibid., 107, pp. 1082-83, italics, mine.
3 From workshop notes, "Mending the Breach," Richard Rohr OFM, Franciscan Center: Tampa, FL, February 7-11,1993.
4 *My Heart's Quest: Collected Writings of Eric Doyle, Friar Minor, Theologian*, edited by Josef Raischl SFO and André Cirino OFM (Canterbury, England: Franciscan International Study Centre, 2005), p. 434.

5 *The Journey into God. A Forty-Day Retreat with Bonaventure, Francis and Clare,* op.cit., pp. 374-78.

6 Ibid., p. 374.

7 *Bonaventure: The Soul's Journey Into God, The Tree of Life, The Life of Saint Francis,* introduction and translation by Ewert Cousins (New York: Paulist Press, 1978), p. 120.

8 Ibid., p. 119. For a detailed study, see St. Bonaventure's *Tree of Life,* Richard Martignetti, OFM (Frati Editori di Quaracchi: Rome, 2004).

9 *The Release of the Spirit,* Watchman Nee (Sure Foundation: Cloverdale, Indiana, 1965), p. 10.

10 *Biblical Meditations for the Easter Season,* Carroll Stuhlmueller CP, (Paulist Press: New York, 1980), p. 87-88.

11 *Clowning In Rome: Contemplation and Ministry,* Henri Nouwen (Image Books: New York, 1979), p. 88.

12 *Clare of Assisi: Early Documents, The Bull of Canonization,* op.cit., 4, p. 240.

13 *St. Francis of Assisi, Omnibus of Sources,* op.cit., *Rule 1223,* pp. 61-62.

14 Ibid., *Letter to a Minister,* p. 110, italics mine.

15 "Mending the Breach," op.cit.

16 *St. Francis and the Song of Brotherhood and Sisterhood,* op.cit., p. 47, italics mine.

17 *Biblical Meditations for Ordinary Time—Weeks 1-9,* Carroll Stuhlmueller, CP (Paulist Press: New York, 1984), p. 130.

18 *The Journey into God: A Forty-Day Retreat with Bonaventure, Francis and Clare,* op.cit., VII:6, p. 402.

19 *The Works of Bonaventure: Soliloquy,* edited by José de Vinck (St. Anthony's Guild: Paterson, NJ, 1966), IV, 4, p. 109.

20 The cross of Christ was probably in the shape of a T, the Tau St. Francis favored. See: *A Doctor at Calvary,* Pierre Barbet (Image Books: Garden City, NY, 1963), p. 62.

21 *The Tau,* Damien Vorreaux, OFM (Franciscan Herald Press: Chicago, 1979), p. 5.

22 See *The Treatise of the Miracles of St. Francis,* 159, where St. Francis heals a man's leg by touching the sore with a stick in the shape of a Tau.

23 *The Tau,* op.cit., p. 10.

The Will of God

1 *St. Francis of Assisi, Omnibus of Sources,* op.cit., *The Little Flowers of St. Francis,* 11, pp. 1323-24; 16, italics mine.

2 "Francis of Assisi at the Crossroads: Elements of a Franciscan Process of Discernment", Anthony Carrozzo OFM in *Review for Religious*, Vol. 41, no. 4, July-August, 1982, pp. 551-556. For those who are interested, the article offers what might be called "a corporate dimension to the Franciscan process of discernment."

3 *St. Francis of Assisi, Omnibus of Sources,* op.cit., 16, pp. 1334-35, adapted and italics mine.

4 Ibid., *1Celano 91*, p. 306 italics mine.

5 *The Works of Bonaventure: The Six Wings of the Seraph,* translated by José de Vinck (St. Anthony Guild Press: Paterson, NJ, 1966), Vol. III, p. 171.

6 *St. Francis of Assisi, Omnibus of Sources,* op.cit., *Earlier Rule* 1:1, p. 31.

7 See also: *A Study of Discernment in the Writings of Francis of Assisi,* Michelle L'Allier, OSF in THE CORD, Vol. 51, No. 5, September October, 2001, pp. 234-241.

8 I also presented this process at a workshop in Assisi (1991) to the vocation directors of the OFM English-speaking Conference for use with prospective vocations.

9 *Bonaventure: Mystical Writings*, Zachary Hayes OFM (Crossroad Publishing Company: New York, 1999), pp. 28-29.

10 Ibid.

11 *The Geste of the Great King: Office of the Passion of Francis of Assisi,* Laurent Gallant, OFM, and André Cirino, OFM (New York: Franciscan Institute Publications, 2001), pp. 221-22, Scripture translations mine.

12 *Franciscan Solitude*, André Cirino, OFM, and Josef Raischl, SFO (New York: Franciscan Institute Publications, 1995), p. 344.

13 *Francis of Assisi at the Crossroads: Elements of a Franciscan Process of Discernment,* op. cit., pp. 552-53.

14 Ibid., adapted.

15 Ibid., p. 554.

16 Ibid.

17 *St. Francis of Assisi, Omnibus of Sources,* op.cit., *Letter to Brother L e o ,* pp. 118-19.

Conclusion

1 *The Journey into God: A Forty-Day Retreat with Bonaventure, Francis and Clare*, op.cit., Prologue, p. 348.

André Cirino OFM is a contemporary Franciscan itinerant preacher whose ministerial experience includes parish work, Franciscan formation and high school education. He also worked at the Little Portion Retreat House for the poor in Bronx, New York for 8 years. He is co-author of the book *Teens Encounter Christ* and edited a journal on the writings of Francis, *In the Womb of the Cave*. He and Josef Raischl SFO have jointly published an anthology on Franciscan Solitude; *The Journey Into God: A Forty-Day Retreat with Bonaventure, Francis and Clare; My Heart's Quest: Collected Writings of Eric Doyle, Friar Minor, Theologian; Three Heroes of Assisi in World War II*; and A *Pilgrimage through the Franciscan Intellectual Tradition*. André and Laurent Gallant OFM have published a prayer book and CD (with Josef Raischl) on St. Francis' Office of the Passion: *The Geste of the Great King*. Their most recent CDs—*Love Holding Love*—are Franciscan mantras drawn from the writings of Saints Francis and Clare of Assisi. Since 1984 André has conducted pilgrimages to Italy, Prague, England, Mallorca, France, Germany and the California Missions for Franciscan Pilgrimage Programs. He lectures at the Franciscan International Study Centre, Canterbury, England.

Visit his website at assisijourney.com